CW01494778

ANIMALS IN ISLAM

First edition. April 15, 2025.

Copyright © 2025 MAA.

ISBN: 979-8230482437

Written by MAA.

Animals in Islam

Chapter 1: In the Name of Mercy

In the Islamic tradition, the very first words a practicing Muslim utters in any act are: *Bismillah ar-Rahman ar-Rahim*—In the name of God, the Most Compassionate, the Most Merciful. These words are not mere formalities; they are a daily reminder of the twin pillars of God's nature: mercy and compassion. They are recited before meals, at the beginning of journeys, when embarking on a task, or even before turning the page of a book. Embedded in these words is the essence of how Muslims are meant to see the world and their place in it.

From the outset, Islam frames the universe as a creation of mercy. The Qur'an refers to itself as a guide and mercy for those who believe, and the Prophet Muhammad (peace be upon him) is repeatedly described as a "mercy to the worlds" (*rahmatan lil-'alamin*). Importantly, that mercy is not confined to human beings. The term "worlds" (*al-'alamin*) encompasses all of creation—plants, animals, even the unseen. It is this expansive understanding that shapes the relationship between Muslims and the animal kingdom.

The Arabic word *rahmah*—mercy—is rooted in the word *rahm*, meaning womb. This linguistic connection conveys a deep emotional and moral sense of care, one that is nurturing and protective. Just as the womb sustains life quietly and consistently, mercy in Islam is not an abstract ideal but a lived practice of gentleness toward all creatures. Animals, in this framework, are not lesser beings; they are living signs of God, integrated into the spiritual and moral architecture of life.

In the Qur'an, animals are described not just as beings with physical form, but as communities—*umamun amthalukum*—nations like you. This powerful phrase appears in Surah Al-An'am (6:38): "There is not an animal in the earth, nor a bird that flies with its wings, but they are communities like you." This verse reorients the human-centered worldview. Animals are not background actors in the human story; they are part of the divine narrative, each with its own dignity, purpose, and order.

Mercy toward animals is not optional; it is required. The Prophet Muhammad taught that a woman who starved a cat to death would be punished in the Hereafter, while another woman who gave water to a thirsty dog was forgiven her sins. These teachings do not merely highlight individual acts of kindness or cruelty—they reflect a theological stance: that animals have spiritual significance and that how one treats them is a reflection of one's faith.

Islam does not grant dominion in the way some other traditions might interpret it. Instead, it offers stewardship—*khilafah*—a role of responsibility rather than superiority. The earth and all its creatures are seen as a trust, an *amanah*, given to humanity not to exploit but to protect. This concept places moral weight on human actions, especially in how we interact with other living beings.

In the natural order described by the Qur'an, animals have a role in praising God, even if humans cannot comprehend it. "Do you not see," the Qur'an says, "that all beings in the heavens and the earth glorify God—even the birds spreading their wings? Each one knows its own prayer and glorification" (24:41). This idea—that animals are conscious in their own way, that they have a relationship with the Divine—is not metaphorical. It is stated as fact, challenging any belief that human intellect alone is the measure of worth.

Within this theological structure, mercy is not sentimentalism. It is law, ethos, and metaphysics all at once. It is the very architecture of divine intention, and it demands a moral response from those who believe. To live *in the name of mercy* is to recognize the sanctity of every creature and to act accordingly—with reverence, care, and humility.

Chapter 2: The Breath of Life

In Islamic thought, the act of creation is never seen as random or mechanical. It is an act of divine will, an unfolding of purpose and order. In the Qur'an, the creation of life is described in vivid and profound terms, with every element of the natural world being a manifestation of God's intent. This includes not only humans but also animals, whose lives are equally imbued with divine purpose.

When God created Adam, He did not merely form him from clay; He breathed His spirit (*ruh*) into him. This divine breath, symbolizing the infusion of life, awareness, and consciousness, was not unique to humans. The Qur'an presents animals as beings who, like humans, are recipients of this sacred breath. In Surah Al-An'am (6:38), God says, "There is no animal on the earth, nor a bird that flies with its wings, but they are communities like you." This verse highlights that animals are not just passive creatures; they are also alive with the breath of life and share a connection with humans in the eyes of the Creator.

The Qur'an continually emphasizes that all living creatures, from the smallest insect to the grandest mammal, are part of the divine creation. They are described as *ayat* (signs), each one bearing witness to God's creativity, power, and mercy. The term *ayat* suggests that animals, just like the natural world at large, have a purpose beyond mere existence. They are living symbols meant to inspire awe, reflection, and gratitude.

Surah An-Nahl (16:5) speaks of animals as creatures designed with multiple benefits: "And He created the cattle for you: in them is warmth and numerous benefits, and of their meat, you eat." This verse not only acknowledges the material benefits animals provide but also calls attention to their essential role in the human experience. They are part of a larger, interconnected system where every creature plays a vital role.

But animals are not merely for human benefit. The Qur'an emphasizes their importance within the natural order. In Surah Al-Baqarah (2:164), it speaks of the signs of God being found in all creatures: "Indeed, in the creation of the heavens and the earth, and the alternation of the night and the day, and the [great] ships which sail through the sea with that which benefits people, and what God has sent down from the heavens of water, giving life thereby to the earth after its lifelessness and dispersing therein every kind of moving creature... are signs for people who use reason."

In these verses, animals are not seen as mere instruments for human use; they are integral parts of God's creation that help sustain the balance of life. The idea of animals as *communities* like humans reinforces the notion that their existence is just as purposeful and significant.

Beyond their role in providing sustenance or service, animals are considered beings of dignity and worth in Islam. They are not seen as commodities or property to be exploited, but rather as fellow creatures with their own place in the cosmos. As the Qur'an highlights, animals, like humans, are part of a larger ecosystem of life, and all are dependent on one another to sustain the order set by God.

The concept of life in Islam is inherently connected to the breath of life given to all living creatures by God. This breath is not a simple physical force; it represents the deeper, spiritual essence that connects every living being to the divine. Animals, through their very existence, reflect this divine energy, and it is in their life, their movements, and their natural behavior that they demonstrate the beauty of creation.

Even the smallest creatures in the Qur'an—bees, ants, and flies—are acknowledged for their unique roles. The story of the ant in Surah An-Naml (27:18), when it warns other ants to seek shelter from the approaching army of Prophet Sulaiman, illustrates that animals have awareness and purpose. The verse conveys the idea that animals are not mere automatons but beings endowed with intelligence and the capacity to respond to their environment in ways that reflect God's wisdom.

The Qur'an also reveals that animals, like humans, have a way of glorifying God. "Do you not see that to God prostrates whatever is in the heavens and whatever is on the earth, and the sun, the moon, the stars, the mountains, the trees, the animals, and many of mankind?" (22:18). This verse further emphasizes the interconnectedness of all creation and the shared purpose of life: the worship of the Creator.

In this light, the breath of life is not just the physical animation of a body, but a divine essence that flows through every living creature. It is the means by which the natural world participates in the divine rhythm of existence. The Qur'an encourages reflection on the behavior of animals as a means to understand the wisdom of God's creation and to cultivate a deeper sense of humility and reverence in human hearts.

By recognizing the breath of life in all creatures, Muslims are reminded to approach the world with a sense of wonder and responsibility. Animals, as part of this sacred order, are to be treated with the same dignity and respect that all of creation deserves.

Chapter 3: The Prophet's Love for Animals

Prophet Muhammad (peace be upon him) exemplified the ideal treatment of animals through both his actions and his teachings. His love for all creatures, great and small, is a central aspect of his life that continues to resonate with Muslims today. The Prophet's interactions with animals were not just acts of kindness; they were reflective of his deeper understanding of God's creation and the moral responsibility humans have toward it.

One of the most notable aspects of the Prophet's relationship with animals was his deep compassion. He often spoke of kindness to animals, emphasizing that good treatment of animals is a reflection of one's faith. He famously said, "Whoever is kind to the creatures of God, he is kind to himself" (Sahih al-Bukhari). This saying reinforces the idea that the treatment of animals is not merely a moral choice but a reflection of spiritual health and compassion.

The Prophet's affection for animals was not limited to domestic pets; it extended to all creatures. One well-known incident involved a camel that the Prophet encountered. This camel was so distressed that it cried out in sorrow when it saw the Prophet. Upon noticing the animal's emotional distress, the Prophet immediately inquired about its well-being and discovered that it had been overworked and neglected by its owner. The Prophet's face filled with concern, and he addressed the owner sternly, saying, "Fear Allah in these animals who cannot speak" (Abu Dawood). This story illustrates the Prophet's sensitivity to the needs and feelings of animals, showing that he did not consider them as mere tools, but as living beings deserving of care.

In another famous story, a woman came to the Prophet, confessing that she had tied up a cat and left it without food or water until it died. The Prophet expressed his displeasure, declaring that she would be punished for her cruelty. He explained that even in something as seemingly small as the treatment of a cat, one's actions carry significant weight in the eyes of God. This teaching serves as a powerful reminder of the spiritual and moral consequences of cruelty to animals in Islam.

Prophet Muhammad's love for animals was also demonstrated in his care for working animals. He treated horses, camels, and other beasts of burden with the utmost respect, ensuring that they were never overworked and always given proper care. He was keen to prevent unnecessary suffering and even instructed his companions to avoid burdening animals with excessive loads. He once said, "Do not overburden your animals, for they are also creatures of Allah" (Sahih Muslim). This directive was a clear reminder that animals, even when used for work, have rights and deserve humane treatment.

The Prophet's love for birds was also evident. A beautiful example of this can be found in the story of the Prophet Muhammad and a nest of birds. One day, while traveling, the Prophet came across a nest of birds that had been disturbed. Upon seeing this, he immediately instructed his companions to be gentle, saying, "Who disturbed the nest of these birds? Return their eggs to them." This act of compassion demonstrated the Prophet's awareness of the delicate balance of nature and his deep concern for the welfare of animals in their natural habitats.

The Prophet's love for animals was not confined to moments of crisis or immediate need; it was woven into the fabric of his daily life. He was known to have a soft spot for cats, and it is even reported that one of his cats, Muezza, was allowed to drink from his water bowl and often sat on his lap during prayer. There are also stories of the Prophet being particularly fond of horses, a common mode of transport during his time. His relationship with horses is not merely that of a rider and animal but one of mutual respect, with the Prophet ensuring they were well-fed, well-cared for, and never overworked.

The Prophet's example showed that animals, like humans, deserve respect and compassion. His teachings emphasized that kindness to animals was a reflection of a Muslim's relationship with God. Every act of gentleness toward an animal, no matter how small, is viewed as an act of charity. The Prophet himself demonstrated that the care for animals was not an isolated act, but part of a broader philosophy of compassion that extended to all aspects of life.

Through his behavior and his teachings, Prophet Muhammad reminded the Muslim community of the moral and spiritual importance of treating animals with care and respect. He believed that kindness to animals was not only an expression of one's character but also an essential part of living in harmony with God's creation.

Chapter 4: Legal and Ethical Frameworks

In Islam, the treatment of animals is governed not only by moral principles but also by a robust legal framework that ensures their protection and humane treatment. Islamic jurisprudence (fiqh) provides a comprehensive guide on how Muslims should interact with animals, drawing on the Qur'an, Hadith (sayings and actions of the Prophet Muhammad), and the interpretations of classical scholars. This legal framework incorporates a blend of ethics, law, and spirituality, all of which emphasize the moral responsibility that humans have toward animals.

The Qur'an lays the foundation for animal rights through numerous verses that not only describe animals as signs of God's creation but also command humans to treat them with compassion and care. For instance, Surah Al-An'am (6:38) asserts that animals are communities like humans, indicating their value in the eyes of God. This verse, along with others, establishes that animals are not merely resources for human use but beings with their own dignity and purpose in the divine order. As such, their treatment is a matter of moral and spiritual accountability.

The ethical treatment of animals is further emphasized in the Hadith. Prophet Muhammad (peace be upon him) provided clear guidance on the appropriate ways to care for animals, from domestic pets to working animals. He instructed his followers to provide animals with proper food, water, and rest, and prohibited cruelty in any form. A well-known Hadith states, "A woman was punished in Hell because of a cat that she had confined until it died. She neither gave it to eat when it was hungry nor let it drink when it was thirsty" (Sahih Muslim). This emphasizes that neglect and abuse of animals are considered grave offenses.

Islamic law, as interpreted by the various schools of thought, offers detailed guidelines on animal rights. The four major Sunni schools of jurisprudence—the Hanafi, Shafi'i, Maliki, and Hanbali—have developed principles that align in many ways but also present some differences in how animals should be treated in various contexts.

The Hanafi School

The Hanafi school of thought emphasizes the concept of *amanah* (trust) in relation to animals. Animals are seen as being entrusted to humans by God, and as such, Muslims are required to fulfill their moral duty of care toward them. According to Hanafi scholars, animals must be treated with respect and kindness, and any form of unnecessary harm is forbidden. The Hanafi school also stresses that animals should be slaughtered in the most humane manner possible, following the halal slaughter method, which minimizes suffering and ensures that the animals are treated with dignity.

The Shafi'i School

The Shafi'i school shares many of the same ethical principles as the Hanafi school but places additional emphasis on the rights of animals in the context of environmental stewardship. Shafi'i scholars have extended the concept of kindness to animals to include the preservation of habitats and the prohibition of overhunting. In their view, Muslims should avoid depleting animal populations and should act as stewards of the earth by protecting the natural environment that animals inhabit.

The Maliki School

The Maliki school places great emphasis on the welfare of animals used for work or transport. According to Maliki jurisprudence, animals that serve humans should not be overburdened or made to endure harsh conditions. The Prophet's Hadith, "Do not overburden your animals," is frequently cited by Maliki scholars to underscore the importance of fairness in the treatment of working animals. The Maliki school also advocates for the humane treatment of slaughtered animals, requiring that they be slaughtered swiftly and with minimal pain.

The Hanbali School

The Hanbali school is perhaps the strictest in terms of animal welfare, requiring the highest standards of care for all animals. Hanbali scholars emphasize the prohibition of cruelty to animals, whether in the form of physical abuse or neglect. The Hanbali school also highlights the spiritual dimension of animal welfare, noting that harming an animal is not only a legal violation but a sin that negatively affects one's standing with God. This school extends the notion of animals as God's creatures with intrinsic value, asserting that they are to be treated with reverence and care.

Animal Slaughter in Islamic Law

One of the most detailed and debated aspects of Islamic jurisprudence regarding animals is the matter of slaughter, particularly in relation to the dietary laws of halal meat. The Qur'an explicitly mentions the proper way to slaughter animals for consumption. In Surah Al-Ma'idah (5:3), it states, "Forbidden to you [for food] are: dead meat, blood, the flesh of swine, and that on which has been invoked the name of other than Allah." This lays the foundation for halal dietary laws, which stipulate that animals must be slaughtered by a Muslim in the name of God, using a sharp instrument to minimize suffering.

Islamic scholars agree that the process of slaughter should be done swiftly and humanely, with the least amount of pain to the animal. The animal should be slaughtered by cutting the throat, windpipe, and blood vessels, allowing the blood to drain from the body. This ensures that the animal does not suffer unnecessarily and that it is treated with dignity throughout the process. There are, however, variations among the different schools of thought regarding the technicalities of slaughter, such as the specific timing and methods used, but all share the underlying principle of minimizing suffering.

Hunting and Treatment of Wild Animals

Islamic jurisprudence also addresses the treatment of wild animals, particularly in the context of hunting. Hunting for sport is generally discouraged, as it is seen as an unnecessary act of cruelty. However, hunting for sustenance is permissible under specific conditions, and hunters must ensure that animals are killed quickly and humanely. Furthermore, any animal that is hunted must be slaughtered in the prescribed halal manner, ensuring that it meets the same standards of respect and care as domesticated animals.

Animal Rights and Environmental Stewardship

A recurring theme in Islamic jurisprudence is the concept of stewardship (*khilafah*) of the earth. Muslims are considered caretakers of the natural world, which includes the responsibility to ensure the welfare of animals and protect their habitats. This notion of environmental stewardship extends to the ethical treatment of animals in farming, the protection of endangered species, and the avoidance of actions that harm the delicate balance of nature.

Islamic scholars have long advocated for the protection of animals in a broader ecological sense. They have encouraged Muslims to be mindful of the impact of human actions on the environment, including deforestation, pollution, and the destruction of animal habitats. By maintaining balance in the natural world, humans honor the trust that God has placed in them as stewards of creation.

Chapter 5: Domesticated Companions

In Islamic tradition, the bond between humans and domesticated animals has always been one of mutual respect and understanding. Animals have long played an essential role in the lives of Muslims, from providing companionship and assistance in daily tasks to offering protection and serving as symbols of grace and beauty. The Prophet Muhammad (peace be upon him) himself was deeply connected to domesticated animals, reflecting the profound respect Islam encourages for these companions.

Cats: Beloved Companions

Among the most beloved of domesticated animals in Islam are cats, a species that has enjoyed a particularly warm place in the hearts of Muslims. Cats are frequently mentioned in the Hadith, with stories that highlight their gentle nature and the Prophet's affection for them. It is reported that the Prophet had a cat named Muezza, whom he adored. One of the most famous stories about Muezza involves the Prophet cutting off a piece of his garment rather than disturbing the cat while it was asleep on his robe. This act of kindness reflects the Prophet's profound respect for the comfort and well-being of his animal companions.

The Prophet Muhammad's fondness for cats has led to their special status in Islam. Cats are considered clean animals, and it is permissible for them to enter homes and mosques. Their presence is welcomed, and they are often seen as symbols of purity and grace. It is also believed that cats have a unique place in the spiritual life of Muslims, with many associating them with good fortune and blessings.

Dogs: Guardians and Helpers

Dogs, while traditionally seen as working animals in Islam, also hold an important role in the lives of many Muslims. Unlike some other cultures, dogs are not viewed as inherently unclean but are respected for their utility and the assistance they provide in various roles, such as guarding property and herding livestock. The Prophet Muhammad (peace be upon him) recognized the value of dogs in his community, particularly in relation to their role in hunting and protection.

It is known that the Prophet allowed the use of dogs for hunting and guarding. The Qur'an also acknowledges the role of dogs, stating in Surah Al-Ma'idah (5:4), "...except what you are able to hunt and slaughter, and your trained dogs, which you train as God has taught you." This highlights the beneficial role of dogs in providing food and security. However, the Prophet also emphasized that dogs should be treated with kindness and not subjected to cruelty. For instance, it is reported that he said, "Whoever kills a dog without a just cause will be punished" (Sahih Muslim). This shows that while dogs are allowed to fulfill specific tasks, their welfare is also a matter of concern.

Dogs in Islam are generally not allowed to enter places of prayer, such as mosques, due to concerns about purity, but they are still regarded as companions that serve essential functions. It is important to note that the teaching of kindness toward dogs is deeply ingrained in the Islamic tradition, with the Prophet Muhammad's own example serving as a guide for Muslims.

Horses: Noble Beasts of Burden

Horses, along with camels, have played a significant role in Islamic history, particularly in warfare and transport. The Prophet Muhammad (peace be upon him) himself was known for his love of horses, considering them noble creatures. Horses were frequently used for battle, travel, and as symbols of strength and honor. The Prophet is reported to have said, "A horse is a noble beast, and it will carry you towards good deeds" (Sunan Abu Dawood). This hadith illustrates not only the practical value of horses but also the respect and reverence that they commanded in Islamic society.

The importance of horses in the early Islamic period cannot be overstated. They were vital for the spread of Islam across vast territories, as they facilitated communication, trade, and military conquest. The Prophet Muhammad (peace be upon him) would often encourage his followers to treat their horses with care and respect, ensuring that they were well-fed, well-groomed, and never overburdened. He famously advised, "Feed your horses before you feed yourselves, for the horses are the means of your strength" (Al-Tabari).

Camels: The Pillars of Early Muslim Society

Camels, like horses, played an indispensable role in the early days of Islam. Known as the "ships of the desert," camels were used for transportation, trade, and sustenance. The Prophet Muhammad (peace be upon him) was intimately familiar with camels, having relied on them for travel throughout the Arabian Peninsula. His fondness for camels was evident, and he often urged his followers to treat them with respect, recognizing their crucial role in the survival and success of early Muslim communities.

In the Hadith, the Prophet Muhammad (peace be upon him) is reported to have said, "Take care of your camels, for they are the creatures that carry your goods and protect you in times of travel" (Sahih al-Bukhari). This emphasis on the camel's essential role in sustaining human life speaks to the deep bond between humans and domesticated animals in Islam. Camels were also used for their milk and meat, providing sustenance for nomadic Bedouins and early Muslims alike. Yet, even as they served these vital functions, the Prophet's teachings on kindness extended to camels as well. He advised against overburdening them or making them suffer unduly.

Other Domestic Animals and the Role of Livestock

Beyond cats, dogs, horses, and camels, Islam recognizes the value and dignity of other domesticated animals, such as sheep, goats, and cows. These animals were essential for early Muslim communities, providing wool, milk, and meat. The Qur'an mentions livestock as blessings from God, calling on humans to be grateful for the sustenance they provide: "And the cattle, He has created them for you. In them are warm garments and numerous benefits, and of them you eat" (Qur'an 16:5).

The treatment of livestock in Islam is governed by a code of ethics that stresses kindness, moderation, and fairness. The Prophet Muhammad (peace be upon him) cautioned against cruelty, warning that animals should not be overworked or treated harshly. It is reported that he said, "Whoever is kind to the creatures of God, he is kind to himself" (Sahih al-Bukhari).

This teaching underscores the fundamental Islamic principle that kindness to animals is not just an act of compassion but a reflection of one's relationship with God.

The Prophetic Example: Treating Animals as Family

What sets the Islamic approach to domesticated animals apart is its holistic view of their status in human society. Islam teaches that animals should not be treated as mere possessions but as living, feeling beings. The Prophet Muhammad (peace be upon him) set the example by treating domesticated animals with the same care and respect as family members. Whether it was his affection for his cat Muezza, his instructions regarding the proper treatment of horses and camels, or his admonishments to treat livestock with kindness, the Prophet's example remains a model for Muslims today.

Chapter 6: Livestock and Labour

In Islamic tradition, livestock have long been considered essential to both the survival and prosperity of human societies. The Qur'an and the Hadith present a profound connection between humans and the animals they rely on for work and sustenance. Livestock such as cattle, camels, goats, and horses are more than mere tools or commodities; they are considered blessings from God, entrusted to humans to be treated with care and respect. Islam emphasizes the balance between utilizing animals for human benefit and ensuring their well-being, maintaining ethical practices in all areas of animal husbandry and labor.

Animals as Partners in Daily Life

Livestock in Islam were not only central to food production but also to daily labor and transport. Camels, horses, and oxen were used for farming, carrying goods, and providing transportation across the harsh terrains of the Arabian Peninsula and beyond. The Prophet Muhammad (peace be upon him) understood the importance of these animals in daily life, and he taught his followers to view them as partners in sustaining human life, rather than simply as tools to be exploited.

The Prophet himself was intimately familiar with the roles these animals played, having relied on them during his travels and in the early expansion of the Islamic community. For instance, camels were essential for desert travel, and horses were used for military purposes. These animals were more than beasts of burden; they were integral to the success of early Islamic society. The Prophet's teachings about their care and treatment were aimed at ensuring that the bond between humans and animals was mutually respectful.

The Ethical Treatment of Working Animals

Islamic teachings stress that animals used for work should not be overburdened or mistreated. The Prophet Muhammad (peace be upon him) emphasized moderation, urging that animals be given appropriate rest and not be subjected to excessive labor. One of the Prophet's famous sayings is, "Do not overburden your animals. They are your partners in your work, and you should be just in your treatment of them" (Sunan Abu Dawood). This guidance serves as a reminder that while animals can be relied upon for their strength and endurance, their well-being must never be compromised.

The concept of justice is central to Islamic ethics, and this extends to the treatment of working animals. The Prophet Muhammad (peace be upon him) advised against overworking animals, stressing that they should not be forced to carry more than their capacity. He once observed a camel that was clearly exhausted and scolded its owner for not showing compassion. This concern for the welfare of working animals is reflected throughout Islamic law, which advocates for fair treatment and the prevention of unnecessary hardship.

Camels: Vital Workers of the Desert

In the early days of Islam, camels were indispensable to the nomadic lifestyle of many Arab tribes. The Prophet Muhammad (peace be upon him) not only relied on camels for transport but also as a source of sustenance, providing milk and meat. In the harsh conditions of the desert, camels were essential for survival. Their ability to withstand extreme heat, travel long distances, and carry heavy loads made them the perfect animals for the desert environment.

The importance of camels in Islamic society is evident in the teachings of the Prophet. He understood the value of these animals not only as carriers of goods but also as creatures deserving of kindness and respect. The Prophet would ensure that camels were properly fed and cared for before embarking on long journeys. He also instructed his followers to treat their camels with kindness and never abuse them for personal gain. "Fear Allah in these animals who cannot speak," he said, highlighting the responsibility humans have toward these loyal companions.

Horses: Strength and Honor in Service

Horses, too, played a critical role in early Islamic society, particularly in warfare. They were symbols of strength, nobility, and courage, often associated with the defense and spread of Islam. The Prophet Muhammad (peace be upon him) had a deep respect for horses, understanding their importance not only as animals of war but as companions that served to elevate human dignity.

In the context of labor, horses were used for transportation and as a means of facilitating trade. The Prophet Muhammad (peace be upon him) ensured that horses were well cared for and provided with adequate food, water, and rest. The Prophet's guidance on the treatment of horses extended beyond military use; it encompassed all aspects of their care. He instructed his companions to ensure that horses were not overworked and that they were treated with the utmost respect. In one of his famous sayings, the Prophet emphasized the nobility of horses: "A horse is a noble beast, and it will carry you toward good deeds" (Sunan Abu Dawood).

Cattle and Sheep: Providers of Sustenance

Cattle, sheep, and goats have also been vital to Muslim communities, serving as sources of milk, meat, and wool. These animals were raised in many parts of the Islamic world and were integral to the agricultural economy. Islam encourages the ethical treatment of these animals, particularly in terms of how they are handled and slaughtered for food. The Prophet Muhammad (peace be upon him) instructed his followers to be kind to cattle and sheep, ensuring that they were not overburdened or treated with cruelty. For example, he warned against causing harm to animals during slaughter, saying, "When you slaughter, do so in the best manner. Let one of you sharpen his knife and give the animal ease in the process" (Sahih Muslim).

Islamic law stipulates that animals raised for food must be provided with adequate shelter, nourishment, and space to roam. The care and well-being of livestock are considered a direct responsibility of their owners, and neglect or mistreatment is not tolerated. The emphasis on humane practices reflects the broader ethical framework of Islam, which encourages compassion and care for all of God's creatures.

Islamic Labor Ethics and the Role of Animals

The ethical treatment of working animals is deeply linked to the broader principles of Islamic labor ethics. In Islam, work is not only a means of earning a living but also an opportunity to serve God by fulfilling one's responsibilities justly and ethically. This includes the treatment of animals. Just as humans are entitled to fair wages and humane treatment in their labor, so too are animals entitled to respect and kindness in their service.

Islamic teachings advocate for a balance between human needs and the welfare of animals. Animals are not to be exploited for labor or sustenance in ways that cause undue harm or suffering. The Qur'an and Hadith stress that while animals are to be used for work, humans are also responsible for their welfare, and any act of cruelty or neglect is seen as a violation of divine commandments. This balance between utility and compassion reflects the broader Islamic worldview, which calls for ethical conduct in all aspects of life, from personal interactions to economic transactions.

Sustainability and Stewardship

The use of livestock in labor also ties into the Islamic principle of stewardship of the earth. Islam teaches that humans are caretakers of God's creation, and this responsibility extends to animals, who are seen as part of the natural balance. The ethical treatment of working animals is not only about kindness but also about preserving the ecological balance that ensures the well-being of all living creatures. Overexploitation, neglect, or harm to animals in the name of labor is seen as a violation of this stewardship.

By encouraging humane practices, Islam seeks to ensure that animals are used in ways that benefit both humans and the creatures themselves. This approach advocates for sustainability in the use of animals for work and food, ensuring that their role in human society does not lead to environmental degradation or the mistreatment of the animals.

Chapter 7: Wildlife in the Qur'an

The Qur'an, the holy book of Islam, does not merely present human beings as the sole recipients of God's blessings but highlights the significance of all living creatures, including wildlife. The verses that mention animals are not only illustrative of the beauty and diversity of creation but also emphasize spiritual, ecological, and ethical lessons. Through these verses, the Qur'an teaches Muslims to appreciate the natural world, recognize the interconnectedness of life, and understand the divine wisdom behind the existence of all creatures.

Animals as Signs (Ayat) of God

One of the central themes in the Qur'an regarding animals is the concept of them being "signs" (ayat) of God's existence, power, and wisdom. The Qur'an repeatedly invites humanity to reflect upon the natural world as a manifestation of divine creation. Animals are not mere creations of the earth but are seen as living signs that point to the greatness and majesty of God.

In Surah An-Nahl (16:5), the Qur'an states: *"And the livestock He has created for you; in them is warmth and numerous benefits, and of them you eat."* This verse highlights the utility of animals in providing sustenance, clothing, and companionship, yet it also encourages believers to reflect on the divine wisdom embedded in the existence of these creatures. Such reflections go beyond material benefits, extending to the recognition that animals are part of a larger, interconnected creation, all of which serve a higher purpose.

Diversity of Wildlife in the Qur'an

The Qur'an mentions a wide range of animals, some of which are domesticated, while others are wild. The mention of different species underscores the diversity and complexity of life on earth. Among the wild animals specifically mentioned in the Qur'an are lions, elephants, bees, and birds. Each of these creatures embodies a unique aspect of creation, offering valuable lessons to those who observe them.

The Elephant: Symbol of Divine Protection

One of the most memorable references to an animal in the Qur'an is the story of the "Army of the Elephant" (Surah Al-Fil), which is named after the elephants that were part of an army sent to destroy the Kaaba in Mecca. This event is depicted as a display of God's protection over the sacred sanctuary. In Surah Al-Fil (105:1-5), it describes how God sent flocks of birds with stones of clay to defeat the army, illustrating the notion that even the largest and most powerful creatures on earth can be rendered powerless when God wills it.

The elephant, despite its immense size and strength, is used in the Qur'an to symbolize the limits of human and animal power in comparison to God's divine will. The story emphasizes God's protection and how, even in the face of overwhelming odds, the balance of power ultimately rests with the Creator.

Bees: Symbols of Productivity and Harmony

Bees hold a particularly significant place in the Qur'an. In Surah An-Nahl (16:68-69), God commands the bees to build their hives in the mountains, trees, and human-made structures. This reference not only illustrates the beauty and efficiency of nature but also highlights the role of bees in the ecosystem as pollinators, contributing to the creation of food and other resources. The verse further states: *"And your Lord inspired the bee, 'Take for yourself among the mountains, houses, and among the trees, and in which they construct.'"* The bee is revered in Islamic tradition as a symbol of productivity, cooperation, and the interdependence of nature.

The verse also alludes to the idea of divine wisdom in the natural processes of the world. Bees, in their seemingly simple actions, are seen as performing a task ordained by God, reminding Muslims of the importance of living harmoniously with the environment and recognizing the interconnectedness of all living beings.

Birds: The Messenger of Wisdom

Birds appear in the Qur'an as symbols of divine wisdom and the beauty of creation. They are often used as metaphors in Islamic poetry and teachings, representing spiritual concepts such as freedom, flight toward God, and the idea of divine revelation. For instance, in the story of Prophet Sulaiman (Solomon), the hoopoe bird plays a pivotal role in delivering important messages from the Queen of Sheba (Surah An-Naml 27:38-40). The bird's role as a messenger reflects its ability to connect the physical and spiritual realms, much like the role of prophets in conveying God's guidance to humanity.

In addition, birds are often portrayed as creatures that express praise to God, as seen in Surah Al-Isra (17:44): *"The seven heavens and the earth, and all that is in them, glorify Him; and there is not a thing that does not glorify Him, but you do not understand their glorification."* This illustrates the idea that all of creation, including wildlife, is constantly in a state of worship, acknowledging God's sovereignty over all things.

Lions: Courage and Strength

The lion, though not as frequently mentioned as other animals in the Qur'an, carries symbolic significance in Islamic thought. Lions are often associated with courage, strength, and the protection of what is sacred. In Islamic tradition, the lion is also linked to the figure of Imam Ali, the cousin and son-in-law of the Prophet Muhammad (peace be upon him), known for his bravery in battle. While the Qur'an does not directly mention lions in a narrative context, their association with these qualities has permeated Islamic culture and spirituality.

Lions also serve as a reminder of the power of God. In Surah Al-A'raf (7:85), the Qur'an uses the metaphor of wild animals and the natural world to emphasize the authority of God in shaping and controlling the forces of nature. The lion, as one of the most powerful creatures, symbolizes the forces of nature that are subjugated by divine will.

Ecological Balance and Ethical Stewardship

The Qur'an consistently emphasizes the theme of balance within the natural world. Every creature, wild or domesticated, has a purpose in maintaining the ecological equilibrium of the planet. Surah Al-An'am (6:141) illustrates this balance: *"It is He who produces gardens trellised and untrellised, date palms, and crops of different shape and taste (its fruits and its seeds), and olives, pomegranates, similar (in kind) and different (in taste). Eat of their fruit when they ripen, but pay the due thereof on the day of its harvest, and waste not by extravagance."* This verse reminds Muslims that while they benefit from the world's resources, they must not be wasteful or exploitative.

The Qur'an teaches that every creature, from the smallest insect to the largest mammal, plays a role in maintaining the delicate balance of nature. In Surah Al-Anbiya (21:107), the Qur'an refers to the Prophet Muhammad (peace be upon him) as a mercy to all worlds, which includes not only humans but also the animals and the environment. Islam encourages stewardship of the earth, advocating for the protection and ethical treatment of wildlife. The Qur'an warns against harming animals or ecosystems, stressing that all creatures are part of God's creation and should be treated with reverence and care.

Chapter 8: Birds of Wisdom

Birds hold a special place in Islamic tradition, both as creatures of nature and as symbols of divine wisdom. From their ability to soar through the skies to their intricate patterns of migration, birds have long been admired for their beauty, grace, and the lessons they offer to those who observe them. In the Qur'an and the Hadith, birds are frequently mentioned as living signs of God's power and mercy, providing profound spiritual and moral lessons.

Birds in the Qur'an: Divine Messengers

In the Qur'an, birds are frequently used as symbols of divine communication, grace, and obedience to God. The most notable example is the story of Prophet Sulaiman (Solomon) and the hoopoe bird. Sulaiman, known for his wisdom and ability to communicate with animals, uses the hoopoe as a messenger. In Surah An-Naml (27:38-40), the hoopoe brings Sulaiman news of the Queen of Sheba and her kingdom. The bird, acting as a divine messenger, highlights the relationship between humans and animals as one that is deeply rooted in communication, trust, and the transmission of knowledge.

The hoopoe's role as a messenger demonstrates the idea that birds, in their flight and movement, connect the earthly realm with the divine. The Qur'anic portrayal of the hoopoe reveals that even the smallest of creatures can carry significant wisdom, and their actions are directed by God's will.

Birds as Symbols of Freedom

Birds are often seen as symbols of freedom, soaring through the sky with grace and ease. Their ability to move freely across vast distances represents a spiritual journey, one that seeks closeness to God. This symbolism is particularly important in Sufi literature, where birds are often used as metaphors for the soul's longing to be united with the divine.

In Sufi poetry, the image of the bird is frequently used to express the yearning of the heart for God. The famous Sufi poet, Rumi, often spoke of birds as symbols of the soul's longing for spiritual fulfillment. In one of his well-known verses, Rumi writes: *"You are not a drop in the ocean. You are the entire ocean in a drop."* This idea mirrors the freedom of birds, who, in their flight, transcend the limitations of the earth and reach toward the infinite. Birds, in this sense, embody the soul's pursuit of enlightenment and spiritual liberation.

The Example of the Nightingale

The nightingale, a bird renowned for its song, is another symbol of divine wisdom in Islamic tradition. Its melodious tunes, which fill the air during the night, are seen as an expression of gratitude and worship to God. In Islamic mysticism, the nightingale is often used as a metaphor for the seeker of divine love, whose heart is filled with longing for God's presence. The bird's song is interpreted as a form of praise, and its solitary call in the quiet of the night represents the soul's quiet devotion to its Creator.

The nightingale's presence in Islamic thought underscores the idea that even the smallest of creatures, through their natural actions, can offer praise to God. The sound of the nightingale's song is an audible reminder of the worship that takes place throughout the universe, whether from humans or animals, in their own ways.

Birds in the Hadith: Lessons in Gratitude and Humility

The Prophet Muhammad (peace be upon him) often used examples from nature to teach his followers important moral lessons, and birds were no exception. In one famous hadith, the Prophet tells the story of a bird that was captured and then freed. Upon being released, the bird flew away, symbolizing freedom and the importance of acting with compassion. This simple story, like many others, was meant to inspire gratitude and humility in the hearts of Muslims, encouraging them to be mindful of their interactions with God's creatures.

The Prophet Muhammad (peace be upon him) also warned against causing harm to birds or any other animals. In a well-known narration, he condemned the practice of killing birds for sport, reminding his followers that all creatures are precious in the eyes of God. This hadith reinforces the Islamic principle of mercy and care for all living beings, encouraging Muslims to treat animals with kindness and respect.

In another hadith, the Prophet Muhammad (peace be upon him) observed a woman who had cruelly imprisoned a cat, and he admonished her for her actions. This principle of compassion towards even the smallest creatures, such as birds, extends to all living beings in Islam. The emphasis is on recognizing that animals, just like humans, are part of the divine order and deserve kindness and respect.

The Migratory Journey: A Metaphor for Spiritual Seeking

One of the most remarkable aspects of birds is their ability to migrate across vast distances, traveling from one place to another in search of sustenance and better conditions. This natural instinct has long been viewed as a metaphor for the human journey of seeking knowledge, truth, and spiritual fulfillment. In the Qur'an, the idea of migration is often used to describe the journey of the believer toward God, a journey that requires perseverance, trust, and guidance from God.

In the same way that birds navigate across oceans, deserts, and mountains, believers are encouraged to persevere on their spiritual journey, trusting that God will guide them through the challenges they face. The Qur'anic imagery of birds migrating across the sky can be seen as a reflection of the soul's continuous striving for spiritual elevation.

The Parable of the Bird and the Drop of Water

A famous parable often cited in Islamic mysticism illustrates the relationship between the bird and its sustenance. It is said that the bird, in its quest for food and sustenance, does not search for it in vain, for God has already determined its sustenance. The bird, trusting in God's provision, seeks what is rightfully meant for it. This parable teaches a profound lesson in trust and submission to God's will. Just as the bird seeks food with patience and diligence, so too should the believer seek spiritual sustenance, trusting that God will provide.

The story of the bird and the drop of water also serves as a reminder that, while humans strive to achieve their goals, ultimate success and fulfillment lie in God's hands. The bird's trust in the divine provision is a model of how believers should trust in God's wisdom and plan for their lives.

Birds in Islamic Art and Culture

Beyond their mention in sacred texts, birds hold an enduring presence in Islamic art and culture. In Islamic calligraphy, tilework, and poetry, birds often appear as symbols of beauty, freedom, and divine inspiration. The intricate designs and vibrant depictions of birds serve to remind Muslims of the fleeting beauty of this world and the eternal beauty of the divine.

The presence of birds in Islamic art also symbolizes the connection between the material world and the spiritual realm. Their depiction often carries spiritual significance, encouraging the observer to contemplate the divine mysteries and the deeper meanings hidden within the natural world.

Chapter 9: Aquatic Life and Halal Seafood

Aquatic life holds a special place in Islamic teachings, often referred to as a sign of God's creation that deserves both appreciation and respect. The Qur'an speaks frequently of the oceans, seas, and their creatures, emphasizing the divine order and the spiritual lessons derived from the waters and the beings within them. While the sea itself is presented as a vast, mysterious domain, filled with wonders, it also provides a way for humanity to reflect on their role as caretakers of the environment and the rules of dietary law, including the consumption of halal seafood.

The Sea as a Sign of Divine Power

The Qur'an references the sea not only as a resource for sustenance but also as a vast, expansive symbol of God's infinite knowledge and power. In Surah Al-Nahl (16:14), God says: *"It is He who made the sea subservient, that ye may eat fresh meat from it and that ye may extract from it ornaments to wear; and thou seest the ships therein that plough the waves, that ye may seek of His bounty, that ye may be grateful."*

This verse highlights the twofold purpose of the sea: providing nourishment and resources while also showcasing the majesty of God's creation. It reminds Muslims that the ocean, with its rich diversity of life, is not just a vast body of water but a sign of divine creativity, which provides sustenance for humanity. The abundant life beneath the sea is a testament to the mercy of God, who created such an environment to meet human needs and to inspire awe.

The Halal Concept in Aquatic Life

In Islamic law, one of the central principles governing what is permissible to eat is the concept of *halal*, meaning that which is lawful or permissible. The rules around halal food, as set out in the Qur'an and the teachings of the Prophet Muhammad (peace be upon him), are intended to ensure that Muslims consume food in a way that is ethical, respectful of God's creation, and aligned with the principles of Islamic law.

The Qur'an provides clear guidelines on the permissibility of consuming aquatic life. In Surah Al-Ma'idah (5:96), it states: *"Lawful to you (for food) are all water creatures and seafood."* This verse is one of the foundational texts that confirm the permissibility of eating seafood. Unlike terrestrial animals, the consumption of marine creatures is generally permitted in Islam, including fish, shellfish, and other sea creatures, provided they are harvested in accordance with Islamic principles.

There is, however, a distinction between different types of aquatic life. According to Islamic scholars, fish are clearly halal, but other creatures like certain types of shellfish, crustaceans, and other marine life have varying rulings, depending on the interpretation of different schools of thought. In general, any aquatic creature that is not harmful or harmful to the environment and is taken lawfully is permissible to consume.

The Ethics of Fishing and Harvesting Marine Life

The ethical dimensions of harvesting aquatic life are emphasized in Islam. Just as with terrestrial animals, there is a responsibility to approach the harvesting of marine creatures with care and respect. The Qur'an encourages moderation in all aspects of life, including the use of natural resources. In Surah Al-A'raf (7:31), God commands: *"O children of Adam! Take your adornment at every masjid and eat and drink, but be not excessive. Indeed, He likes not those who commit excess."*

This verse applies to both food and the way in which resources are obtained. While fishing and eating seafood are permissible, overfishing and harming marine ecosystems are discouraged. Islam emphasizes sustainability, ethical treatment of the environment, and ensuring that the act of harvesting from the sea does not lead to depletion or environmental harm.

Moreover, the act of fishing itself is seen in a spiritual light. As an activity that requires patience, skill, and reliance on God's provision, it is a reminder of humanity's dependence on the Creator. Fishing, when practiced with the intention of fulfilling a need, becomes an act of gratitude and submission to the will of God.

Aquatic Creatures as Signs of God's Majesty

The Qur'an frequently speaks about aquatic creatures as signs of God's creative power. In Surah Al-Anbiya (21:30), it mentions: *"And We made from water every living thing. Then will they not believe?"* This verse reflects the interconnectedness of all life with water, which is the source of existence for both marine and terrestrial life. It serves as a reminder that water and its creatures are not mere accidents of nature but are intricately designed and sustained by God's will.

The various creatures of the sea, from the smallest fish to the largest whales, embody the vastness and complexity of God's creation. Muslims are encouraged to reflect on the wonders of the ocean and its creatures, not only as a means of sustenance but as a source of contemplation about God's greatness and the diversity of life He has created.

The Concept of Respecting Marine Life

Islamic teachings also stress the importance of respecting all forms of life, including aquatic animals. Just as Muslims are forbidden from causing unnecessary harm to land animals, the same respect is due to marine life. In a well-known hadith, the Prophet Muhammad (peace be upon him) said: *"Do not kill a living creature, for it is an act of tyranny."* This includes all living beings, whether on land or in water.

In addition, the Prophet Muhammad (peace be upon him) advised kindness toward animals, including marine creatures. Although he did not provide specific instructions about aquatic life, the broader principles of mercy and respect for living beings would apply. Whether one is fishing or consuming seafood, the spirit of the teachings is clear: no animal should suffer unnecessarily, and all creatures should be treated with dignity.

Marine Life and Spiritual Reflection

The sea, with its vast expanse and mysterious depths, is also a place for spiritual reflection. In Islamic tradition, water is seen as a purifier, both physically and spiritually. The act of immersing oneself in water for ritual purification (wudu) is an important practice in Islam, and it symbolizes both physical and spiritual cleanliness. In a similar manner, the life within the sea, with its purity and the abundance of creation, offers a reminder of the divine grace that sustains life.

The unpredictability and vastness of the ocean also symbolize the mysteries of God's knowledge. Just as one cannot fully comprehend the depths of the sea, one cannot fully understand the complete wisdom of God's creation. The sea, like all aspects of nature, invites contemplation and humility, encouraging believers to recognize that they are but small parts of a much larger creation that is constantly sustained by the will of God.

Chapter 10: The Silent Testimony

In the Islamic worldview, all creatures, whether human or animal, are seen as part of a vast, interconnected creation that testifies to the greatness of God. While humans are endowed with speech and intellect, animals, though silent in the human sense, provide a testimony to God's existence, power, and mercy through their mere existence and actions. The concept of animals as silent witnesses to divine truth plays an important role in Islamic thought, challenging human beings to reflect on the subtle but profound signs of God's presence throughout the natural world.

The Qur'an: Animals as Signs (Ayat)

The Qur'an describes animals as *ayat*—signs of God. These creatures, in their variety, beauty, and function, are not simply part of the natural order but represent divine wisdom and intent. The very existence of animals is an act of creation that echoes God's creative will. As the Qur'an states in Surah An-Nahl (16:49-50): *"And to Allah belongs whatever is in the heavens and whatever is on the earth; all are to Him devoutly obedient. And it is He who created the heavens and the earth in six days and then established Himself above the Throne. You have not besides Him any protector or intercessor, so will you not be reminded?"*

In this verse, the submission of all creatures, including animals, to the will of God is clear. Their very obedience to natural laws—whether in their migration patterns, their modes of communication, or their reproductive processes—serves as a silent testimony of God's power and the order He has established in the universe.

The Spiritual Reflection of Animals' Actions

While animals may not speak or communicate in the human sense, their behaviors and instincts reflect the divine order in ways that humans can learn from and contemplate. The Prophet Muhammad (peace be upon him) is reported to have said: *"There is no creature that does not glorify Allah, but you do not understand their glorification."* (Sahih al-Bukhari). This narration reveals that every action of an animal, from the movement of a bird to the actions of an ant, can be seen as a form of worship, a testimony to the Creator, even if humans cannot comprehend it fully.

Animals' instincts, such as the migration of birds or the migration of marine creatures across oceans, reflect an innate obedience to God's commands. These behaviors speak volumes, especially in a world where human beings, endowed with intellect and speech, often struggle to live in harmony with divine will. The silent testimony of animals in their daily acts, whether they are foraging for food, nurturing their young, or following instinctive migratory paths, reminds humans of the divine order that is beyond the complexities of human life.

Philosophical Reflections on the Soul of Animals

Classical Islamic scholars, such as Al-Ghazali and Ibn Sina, discussed the nature of the animal soul and its relationship to God. While the Islamic tradition maintains that animals do not possess the same level of reason or intellectual capacity as humans, they are still seen as sentient beings with a form of soul that is connected to the Creator. Their souls testify to the divine presence in a way that is subtle, often perceived not through words, but through their actions and existence.

In Al-Ghazali's *Ihya' Ulum al-Din*, he reflects on the idea that animals, by virtue of their actions and behaviors, demonstrate a kind of spiritual awareness that is rooted in their instinctual submission to God's commands. The philosopher Ibn Sina similarly argued that the souls of animals, while not rational in the human sense, are no less a testament to God's creative power. He suggests that animals are not simply automatons; they are living beings whose existence testifies to the divine unity and the interconnectedness of life.

Animals as Silent Witnesses on the Day of Judgment

In Islamic eschatology, animals are granted a unique role in the afterlife. On the Day of Judgment, animals will be resurrected and stand before God, where they will receive justice. They will be judged not for their actions, as humans are, but for the treatment they received during their lives. According to a hadith narrated by Abu Huraira, the Prophet Muhammad (peace be upon him) said: *"The rights of animals will be given to them on the Day of Judgment. The animal will be given its full rights, and the oppressors will have to answer for their wrongdoings."* (Sunan Abu Dawood).

The resurrection of animals and their right to divine justice underscores the idea that every creature, even those who cannot speak, has rights and will be held accountable. This serves as a powerful reminder for Muslims that animals are not mere objects or commodities but are sentient beings with inherent value in the eyes of God. Their silence, rather than indicating a lack of presence or significance, signifies their submission to the Creator and their unique role in the grand narrative of creation.

The Testimony of Animals in the Qur'anic Stories

In several Qur'anic stories, animals play pivotal roles as silent witnesses to divine truth and providence. In the story of Prophet Ibrahim (Abraham), when he is thrown into the fire, it is the animals of the land and sky who, in their own way, bear witness to the miracle of his survival. Similarly, the story of Prophet Musa (Moses) and his encounter with Pharaoh's magicians is accompanied by the miraculous presence of animals, such as the serpent that Moses transforms with God's permission. These animals, though not speaking in the human sense, are part of the greater tapestry of signs that point to the divine.

The Qur'an also mentions the role of animals in supporting prophets, like the use of the camel in the journey of Prophet Muhammad (peace be upon him) during the Hijrah (migration), which is another example of the animals' silent but significant participation in the unfolding of God's plan.

The Testimony of Animals in Our Lives

The role of animals as silent testimonies is not only limited to their presence in sacred texts or their actions in the afterlife but extends to their interaction with humans in the everyday world. The Prophet Muhammad (peace be upon him) often spoke of the importance of treating animals with respect and kindness.

He is reported to have said: *"Whoever is kind to the creatures of God, he is kind to himself."* (Sahih Muslim).

When we interact with animals, we are reminded of our duty to care for God's creation. The silent testimony of animals calls humans to reflect on their own behavior and ethics. Animals do not speak in words, but through their actions, needs, and existence, they reflect the divine order and encourage us to act with wisdom, compassion, and responsibility.

Chapter 11: Animal Welfare in Islamic Civilization

Throughout history, Islamic societies have demonstrated a unique commitment to animal welfare, guided by the teachings of the Qur'an and the Hadith. This commitment transcended the theoretical realm and manifested in practical systems that promoted compassion and respect for animals, both in everyday life and within the structure of the broader community. The integration of these teachings into the social, legal, and environmental fabric of Islamic civilization created a legacy of humane treatment that extended well beyond simple theological ideals.

One of the earliest examples of animal welfare in Islamic history is the establishment of **animal hospitals**. During the reign of the Abbasid Caliphate in the 8th and 9th centuries, Baghdad became home to one of the first known veterinary schools. These hospitals provided care for horses, camels, and other working animals, ensuring that they were treated for illness and injury with the same attention and diligence as human patients. The inclusion of animals in medical care represented a practical application of the Islamic concept of mercy, which recognizes the suffering of all sentient beings, not just humans.

The concept of **waqf** (charitable endowments) also played a significant role in animal welfare during Islamic civilization. Waqf institutions funded public services, and some were specifically set up to care for animals in need. For example, stray cats in cities like Cairo and Istanbul were provided food and shelter through waqf foundations. This initiative was grounded in the idea of creating a balance between human needs and the well-being of animals that shared urban spaces with people. Such acts of kindness were considered acts of piety and charity, rewarding those who contributed to the welfare of animals.

Public **fountains and water systems** were another significant aspect of animal welfare in the Islamic world. These structures were built with the dual purpose of providing water for both humans and animals. In the bustling marketplaces of medieval Islamic cities, public fountains provided water for horses, camels, and livestock, ensuring that animals were not deprived of essential resources while on long journeys or working in harsh conditions. The Qur'anic command to treat animals with dignity was mirrored in these public works, which demonstrated a commitment to the physical well-being of animals in the context of urban life.

Islamic rulers, throughout history, were often guided by the principles of justice and compassion toward animals. Under the rule of the Ottoman Empire, a **royal decree** was issued that prohibited the mistreatment of animals, ensuring that the public was held accountable for their actions. The Ottoman legal system included provisions for protecting animals from cruelty, such as regulating the treatment of oxen used for farming and ensuring that animals were not overworked or poorly fed. Similarly, **regulations on the use of working animals** in agriculture and trade emphasized the humane treatment of beasts of burden.

Zoological gardens, or early forms of zoos, were also prominent in Islamic civilization, particularly in cities like Damascus and Cairo. These institutions served as both a means of preserving species and a site for public education on animal behavior and biodiversity. The gardens were designed not only to showcase the beauty and diversity of creation but also to emphasize the importance of respecting the creatures that populate the earth. In these gardens, animals were carefully cared for, and the public was encouraged to observe them with reverence rather than as mere spectacles for amusement.

The Islamic contributions to animal welfare were also evident in the **treatment of pets and domesticated animals**. Cats, in particular, held a special place in Islamic societies. The Prophet Muhammad's love and respect for cats were well-known, and their role in controlling pests was highly valued. Cats were often treated with reverence, and they were cared for in households and public spaces. Historical records from the Islamic world often describe how cats were given food and shelter, and the punishment for mistreating them was harsh. Similarly, dogs, while not kept as pets in the same manner as cats, were respected for their role in hunting, guarding, and herding, with proper care and attention given to their health and well-being.

The ethical treatment of animals was not confined to domesticated species but extended to wildlife as well. **Hunting regulations** in Islamic civilization were stringent, with a focus on sustainable practices that ensured the preservation of wildlife. Hunting for sport was discouraged, and animals were never to be hunted for mere pleasure. This respect for wildlife was evident in Islamic art and literature, where animals were depicted not as trophies but as symbols of the natural balance that governed creation.

From the establishment of veterinary care to the creation of charitable foundations dedicated to animal welfare, Islamic civilization offered a model of compassionate coexistence with animals. This legacy remains an inspiring example of how religious principles can guide practical efforts to protect and honor the lives of all creatures, promoting a deep sense of responsibility that stretches far beyond human needs.

Chapter 12: Slaughter and Sanctity

In Islamic teachings, the act of slaughtering an animal holds profound significance, transcending mere physical necessity. It is intertwined with spirituality, ethics, and a deep sense of respect for God's creation. While animals are provided as sustenance, their lives are regarded as sacred, and the manner in which they are slaughtered must adhere to strict guidelines that ensure their dignity and minimize unnecessary suffering. This chapter explores the Islamic approach to slaughter, focusing on the sanctity of the act, the importance of intention, and the ethical principles that govern it.

The Concept of Halal Slaughter

In Islam, the concept of *halal* (permissible) slaughter is rooted in the belief that all actions, including the act of taking a life for food, should align with God's will. The Qur'an and the Hadith provide clear guidance on the process, emphasizing the need for ethical treatment, the humane treatment of the animal, and the correct performance of rituals. In Surah Al-Ma'idah (5:3), the Qur'an states: *"This day I have perfected for you your religion and completed My favor upon you and have approved for you Islam as religion. So, whoever is forced by hunger with no inclination to transgression—indeed, Allah is Forgiving and Merciful."*

The act of slaughter is considered a part of the worship of God, and it must be done with reverence. The animal should be slaughtered by invoking the name of God (Bismillah) and making the declaration *Allahu Akbar* ("God is the Greatest") before the cut is made. This ritual signifies that the life being taken is not the arbitrary decision of man but is done in accordance with divine will.

The Importance of Minimizing Suffering

One of the core principles in Islamic slaughter is the obligation to minimize the animal's suffering. The Prophet Muhammad (peace be upon him) said: *"Verily, Allah has prescribed excellence in all things. So, when you kill, kill in the best manner. And when you slaughter, slaughter in the best manner."* (Sahih Muslim). This hadith emphasizes that the humane treatment of animals extends to the process of slaughter itself, ensuring that the animal is treated with care and respect until its last moments.

The method of slaughtering in Islam is designed to be swift and efficient. The throat, windpipe, and blood vessels are to be severed, which ensures the rapid loss of consciousness and the swift death of the animal, while allowing the blood to drain from the body. This method is not only believed to reduce pain but also to ensure that the meat remains pure and free from contamination.

The Role of Intention and Consciousness in Slaughter

In Islam, intention (*niyyah*) plays a pivotal role in every action, including slaughter. The act of slaughtering an animal is not simply a mechanical process—it is a spiritual act that requires consciousness and mindfulness. Before slaughter, the individual must recite the name of God and make the intention to slaughter for the purpose of nourishment, acknowledging that the animal is a gift from God.

The importance of intention is underscored in the following hadith, in which the Prophet Muhammad (peace be upon him) said: *"Actions are judged by their intentions, and each person will be rewarded according to what they intended."* (Sahih Bukhari). This principle emphasizes that the act of slaughtering is not simply about meeting a dietary need but also about recognizing the sanctity of life, aligning the act with gratitude to the Creator.

The Ethical Dimensions of Slaughtering for Food

In Islam, every part of the animal must be treated with respect, from the moment of slaughter to the preparation of its meat for consumption. Islamic law dictates that the act of slaughter must be done with a sense of accountability to God and to the animal. Every individual who partakes in the process, whether as a slaughterer or as someone consuming the meat, is bound by an ethical responsibility.

Islamic ethics regarding slaughter also extend to the humane handling of animals prior to slaughter. The Prophet Muhammad (peace be upon him) is reported to have said: *"Do not sharpen your knife in front of the animal, and do not slaughter one animal in front of another."* (Sahih Muslim). This prohibition aims to reduce anxiety and stress for the animals, ensuring that they are not subjected to unnecessary fear or harm before they are slaughtered.

Moreover, Islam emphasizes that animals should not be overburdened or mistreated at any stage of their life. The physical condition of the animal at the time of slaughter must also be considered, as Islam prohibits the slaughter of an animal that is injured, sick, or suffering from unnecessary distress.

Ritual Slaughter and its Significance in Community and Worship

The practice of slaughtering animals is not confined solely to the individual act of consumption; it also holds a collective and communal significance in Islam. One of the most important occasions for slaughter is the celebration of *Eid al-Adha*, when Muslims around the world commemorate the willingness of Prophet Ibrahim (Abraham) to sacrifice his son in obedience to God's command. During *Eid al-Adha*, the slaughter of animals, usually sheep, goats, cows, or camels, is not only an act of devotion but a means of sharing blessings with the less fortunate. The meat from the sacrifice is distributed among family members, friends, and those in need, ensuring that the wealth generated through sacrifice benefits the broader community.

The ritual act of sacrifice during *Eid al-Adha* serves as a reminder of submission to the will of God and the selflessness inherent in giving. The act of sharing the sacrificial meat also emphasizes the interconnectedness of the Muslim community, the importance of charity, and the collective responsibility of ensuring that no one in the community is left in need.

Animal Welfare and Accountability Before God

In Islam, every act of kindness toward animals is considered a means of drawing closer to God. The concept of *ihsan* (excellence) in the treatment of animals is central to this idea. Whether it is through the act of feeding, caring for, or even slaughtering, Muslims are urged to maintain a level of excellence in how they treat animals at all times.

The Prophet Muhammad (peace be upon him) frequently reminded his followers of their duties to animals. One of the most famous narrations about animal welfare comes from a hadith in which the Prophet speaks of a woman who was punished for locking a cat in a cage without food or water. He said: *"She is in Hell because she imprisoned it until it died, and she did not give it to eat or drink when it was hungry or thirsty."* (Sahih Bukhari). This narrative highlights that cruelty toward animals is a serious offense in Islam and that those who fail to treat animals with kindness and respect will be held accountable before God.

The accountability that humans face for how they treat animals extends to the act of slaughter itself. A person who engages in slaughter must do so with the knowledge that their actions will be scrutinized on the Day of Judgment. This reinforces the idea that every act—whether seemingly mundane or profound—holds spiritual significance and must be performed with the awareness that it is done in the sight of God.

Chapter 13: Sin Against the Speechless

In Islam, every creature, regardless of its ability to speak or communicate in human terms, holds inherent value and dignity. The silent creatures of the world—animals—are often vulnerable, and their lack of speech does not make them any less significant in the eyes of God. The teachings of Islam emphasize the sacredness of all life, and mistreatment of animals, particularly those who cannot voice their suffering, is seen as a serious moral failing. This chapter explores the ethical and spiritual implications of cruelty towards animals in Islam, focusing on the responsibility that Muslims have in protecting and caring for the speechless beings that coexist with humanity.

The Responsibility of Compassion

Islam places a profound emphasis on compassion, a virtue that extends to all of creation, not just to human beings. The Qur'an and Hadith provide clear guidance on the treatment of animals, with numerous teachings that urge kindness, mercy, and justice in dealing with all creatures. The Prophet Muhammad (peace be upon him) is known to have said: *"Whoever is kind to the creatures of God, he is kind to himself."* (Sahih Muslim). This hadith reflects the interconnectedness between humanity and the natural world, underscoring the idea that cruelty to animals is not only a violation of their rights but also a form of self-harm for the individual who commits it.

Animals, as God's creatures, are to be treated with the same level of respect and dignity that is expected in human interactions. This is particularly crucial because, unlike humans, animals cannot defend themselves or call for help when they are in pain or distress. Islam teaches that humans are stewards (*khalifah*) of the earth, and this role comes with a sacred responsibility to protect all living beings from harm.

Cruelty as a Sin in the Qur'an and Hadith

The Qur'an frequently addresses the topic of injustice, and this includes cruelty towards animals. In Surah Al-An'am (6:141), the Qur'an instructs: *"And He it is who produces gardens trellised and untrellised, date palms, and crops of different shape and taste (its fruits and its seeds), and olives, and pomegranates, similar (in kind) and different (in taste). Eat of their fruit when they ripen, but pay the due thereof on the day of its fruit, and waste not by extravagance. Verily, He likes not Al-Musrifun (those who waste by extravagance)."* While this verse primarily speaks to human consumption, the broader context of the Qur'an emphasizes a responsible and ethical approach to all consumption, which includes how animals are treated before they become part of the human food chain.

The hadiths of the Prophet Muhammad (peace be upon him) further highlight the severity of cruelty to animals. One well-known narration tells of a woman who was condemned to hellfire because she imprisoned a cat, neither feeding it nor allowing it to find food on its own. The Prophet (peace be upon him) said: *"She is in Hell because she confined it until it died, and she did not give it to eat or drink when it was hungry or thirsty."* (Sahih Bukhari). This severe punishment emphasizes the weight of responsibility that Muslims have in how they treat animals, particularly in cases where cruelty is intentional or neglect is evident.

The Concept of *Ihsan* (Excellence) and Mercy

In Islam, *ihsan* (excellence) is a central concept that applies to every aspect of life, including how one interacts with animals. The Prophet Muhammad (peace be upon him) taught his followers to perform acts of kindness with excellence, and this includes the treatment of animals. Whether feeding, caring for, or even slaughtering, Muslims are urged to do so in the most compassionate and merciful manner.

The idea of *ihsan* also extends to the protection of animals from harm. Islam encourages the idea of mercy toward all creatures, and the Prophet Muhammad (peace be upon him) made it clear that mercy is one of the greatest qualities a believer can possess. One well-known narration states: *"Whoever is merciful even to a sparrow, God will be merciful to him on the Day of Judgment."* (Sunan al-Kubra). This hadith reinforces the connection between mercy toward animals and the mercy a person will receive from God.

Animals, being part of God's creation, should be treated with kindness and respect, even when they are used for labor or food. The spirit of *ihsan* demands that Muslims take care to avoid inflicting unnecessary pain or hardship on animals. Whether it is the way an animal is kept, transported, or slaughtered, each step should be done with the utmost care, ensuring that cruelty is avoided at all costs.

The Impact of Cruelty on the Soul

In Islamic teachings, the consequences of cruelty extend beyond the material world. The treatment of animals, particularly those who cannot speak up for themselves, is seen as a reflection of a person's moral and spiritual state. Cruelty to animals is a sign of a hardened heart, lacking the compassion and empathy that Islam encourages. In fact, one of the reasons for spiritual purification in Islam is to soften the heart and increase one's awareness of the suffering of others, both human and animal.

The Prophet Muhammad (peace be upon him) cautioned that a person who is cruel to animals will face divine retribution. A well-known hadith narrates: *"A man was punished in Hell for starving a dog to death. He was condemned to Hell because he did not give it to drink when the dog was thirsty."* (Sahih Muslim). This story serves as a stark reminder of the spiritual consequences of mistreating animals. The sin of cruelty is not just a matter of social justice but also has eternal ramifications, as it is viewed as a violation of the moral order that Islam seeks to cultivate.

The Moral Test: Accountability to God

The treatment of animals serves as a moral test for Muslims, testing their adherence to the values of kindness, justice, and mercy that are central to Islam. While humans may not always fully understand or appreciate the lives of animals, their treatment is a measure of how closely they follow the path of righteousness outlined in the Qur'an and Hadith.

The act of harming an animal, whether intentionally or through neglect, is seen as a violation of the trust that God has placed in human beings as caretakers of His creation. As stewards of the earth, Muslims are not simply allowed to take from nature for their benefit, but are required to do so with mindfulness and responsibility, ensuring that the rights of animals are upheld and their welfare is safeguarded.

The teachings of Islam consistently reinforce the idea that animals, like humans, are part of God's creation and deserve respect, dignity, and kindness. Cruelty to animals is viewed not only as a violation of their rights but as a sin against God, who has entrusted humanity with the responsibility of safeguarding His creation. Every act of kindness toward animals is a step toward spiritual purification, and every act of cruelty is a reminder of the need to repent and seek forgiveness.

Chapter 14: The Role of Animals in Eschatology

In Islamic eschatology, animals hold a significant place, not only in the context of the present world but also in the life after death. The Qur'an and Hadith offer insight into how animals will be treated in the afterlife, and their role is tied to the ultimate divine justice that will prevail on the Day of Judgment. While human beings are central to many eschatological discussions, animals are also integral to the final reckoning, reflecting the comprehensive scope of divine justice.

The Qur'an teaches that all creatures, including animals, are **accountable** to God in their own way. In Surah Al-An'am (6:38), it is stated, "There is no creature on earth nor a bird that flies with its wings but they are communities like you." This verse emphasizes that animals, like humans, are part of a divine order and will be judged according to their purpose and actions, which are understood within the framework of their creation. Their lives, while different from humans, are equally valued in the eyes of God.

On the Day of Judgment, animals will not be held accountable for sin, as they are considered free from moral responsibility in the same way as young children. Instead, animals will be judged based on how they were treated by humans. In one well-known Hadith, Prophet Muhammad (peace be upon him) stated, **"On the Day of Resurrection, the rights of animals will be fulfilled. The goat with the horns will complain to Allah about the goat without horns that caused it to be harmed."** This Hadith suggests that animals will have the opportunity to seek justice for any harm or mistreatment they experienced in the world. Their right to justice, as granted by God, will be upheld on that day.

The **resurrection of animals** on the Day of Judgment is also a key concept in Islamic eschatology. It is believed that animals will be resurrected, and their treatment by humans will be a source of divine reckoning. The animals' resurrection is not for the purpose of rewarding or punishing them, as they are free from moral wrongdoing. Rather, their resurrection serves as a means for them to receive divine justice for any wrongs they endured during their earthly existence. This reinforces the idea that God's justice encompasses all of creation, regardless of species.

A significant theme in Islamic eschatology is that **all creation will testify** on the Day of Judgment. The Qur'an mentions in Surah Al-Qiyama (75:13-14), "On that Day, the people will be made to see what they have done; the disbeliever will wish that he were dust." This verse, though referring to human beings, is often interpreted to include all creatures that God has created. In a Hadith narrated by Ibn Majah, it is stated that **"The animals will be gathered together on the Day of Judgment, and they will be called to account for the way they were treated. Once the reckoning is completed, Allah will allow them to do as they wish, and they will be turned into dust."** This emphasizes that animals, too, will experience justice, and their treatment in life will be accounted for.

The **reward and punishment of animals** on the Day of Judgment are tied to how they were treated by human beings. In one story, a woman is said to have been punished for her cruelty to a cat, which she had confined without providing it food or water. Conversely, another woman who cared for a thirsty dog was rewarded by Allah for her act of kindness. These stories highlight the divine principle that the treatment of animals can directly affect one's standing before God, reinforcing the importance of mercy and compassion in daily life.

Furthermore, some scholars have posited that **the presence of animals in paradise** serves as a symbol of divine mercy. While the exact nature of animals in paradise is not explicitly detailed, it is commonly understood that animals will be present in the Hereafter. This presence may not be in the same form as earthly life, but animals, as part of God's creation, will undoubtedly play a role in the eternal bliss of the righteous. In this regard, animals' symbolic role in paradise may serve as a reminder of the interconnectedness of all beings, where no creation is left behind.

The theme of animals in eschatology also brings a deeper understanding of **divine mercy**. The fact that animals, despite their lack of moral accountability, will be fully acknowledged and their rights upheld reflects the profound mercy of God. This is a mercy that extends beyond human beings to all living creatures, showing that the Creator's compassion does not discriminate based on species.

Islamic eschatology, therefore, provides a vision of the afterlife in which animals, as integral parts of the divine creation, are treated with the same care and justice that God extends to all creatures. Their resurrection and the fulfillment of their rights on the Day of Judgment serve as a powerful reminder of the comprehensive nature of divine justice. In the end, the presence of animals in the eschatological narrative emphasizes the idea that all of creation, regardless of its form, is important and deserving of respect in the sight of God.

Chapter 15: Islamic Environmental Ethics

The ecological balance present in the natural world is described in the Qur'an as a sign of divine wisdom. Each creature, plant, river, mountain, and cloud is part of a delicately calibrated order—one that is maintained by divine decree and upheld by the mutual interdependence of all living things. This balance, referred to in the Qur'an as *mīzān*, is not only physical but also moral, establishing an equilibrium that humans are entrusted to respect.

Islamic teachings embed environmental responsibility in theological foundations. The earth is referred to repeatedly as a trust (*amānah*) given to humanity, a place that must be inhabited with humility and care. The human role as *khalīfa*—vicegerent—on earth carries not a license to exploit, but a duty to preserve. The Qur'an does not depict dominion as conquest, but as stewardship anchored in justice (*'adl*) and mercy (*rahmah*).

The Prophet Muhammad (peace be upon him) cultivated an ethos of sustainable living long before such terms existed. He advised against waste, even in the use of water for ablution when standing beside a flowing river. His life reflected simplicity and a deep reverence for the natural world. He planted trees, cared for greenery, and spoke of the reward for those who do the same. In a well-known narration, he said: "If a Muslim plants a tree or sows seeds, and then a bird, or a person, or an animal eats from it, it is regarded as a charitable gift (sadaqah)."

Forests, animals, and even the soil are granted a kind of legal and spiritual status in Islamic jurisprudence. Classical scholars discussed the impermissibility of destroying habitats unnecessarily, emphasized the protection of grazing land, and supported public access to clean water and shade. Jurists in Andalusia and the Ottoman Empire upheld regulations preventing overgrazing and water pollution.

The Qur'anic worldview does not see nature as inert. It is expressive, praising God in its own language. Trees bow, thunder glorifies, and the sun and moon follow their prescribed courses in obedience. Human beings, though equipped with reason and free will, are cautioned not to transgress the limits set by this divine rhythm.

Pollution, overconsumption, and deforestation are not merely environmental concerns but moral disruptions. They represent a failure to fulfill the role of *khalīfa*. Qur'anic verses that describe the corruption (*fasād*) that spreads across land and sea due to human hands serve as both diagnosis and warning. This corruption affects animals, the climate, and communities dependent on fragile ecosystems.

Islamic environmental ethics does not separate the spiritual from the physical. Planting a tree is an act of faith. Conserving water is an act of worship. Treating animals with gentleness is a reflection of tawḥīd—the recognition of God's unity and presence in all aspects of creation. In this holistic view, ecological consciousness is inseparable from religious consciousness.

The early Muslim world saw the establishment of gardens, protected forests, and water distribution systems guided by this ethical framework. Cities like Fez and Isfahan had intricate systems for managing waste and irrigation. Waqf endowments were set up to fund fountains for birds and shelters for working animals. Environmental well-being was linked to social justice, spiritual health, and legal responsibility.

As environmental degradation accelerates in the modern age, these foundational Islamic teachings provide timeless guidance. The tradition does not only support the conservation of resources; it elevates such acts to the realm of sacred duty.

Chapter 16: Modern Challenges and Islamic Responses

The contemporary world presents ethical dilemmas that were unimaginable in the early Islamic period. Industrialization, technological advancement, and globalization have reshaped the human-animal relationship in ways that raise urgent moral questions. From the treatment of animals in factory farms to their use in genetic experimentation, modern practices often clash with the foundational Islamic values of mercy, balance, and accountability.

Factory farming is perhaps one of the most pressing concerns. Animals raised for meat, dairy, and eggs are frequently kept in overcrowded conditions, subjected to stress, and deprived of natural behaviors. This system, designed for efficiency, neglects the welfare of the creatures it relies upon. The Islamic requirement that animals be treated with kindness before slaughter is incompatible with such industrial methods. Classical jurists emphasized that even in lawful slaughter, the animal must not see the blade, must be given water, and must not be harmed before its time. These principles are not honored in mechanized slaughterhouses, where the act of taking life is divorced from the spiritual mindfulness that Islamic tradition demands.

The extinction of species is another challenge. Human activity—through habitat destruction, pollution, and overhunting—has accelerated the disappearance of countless animal species. Islam's concept of *fasād*, or corruption on the earth, includes this kind of disruption. The Qur'an warns that "corruption has appeared on land and sea because of what the hands of people have earned" (30:41). This verse echoes with deeper urgency in an era of mass deforestation, ocean degradation, and biodiversity loss. The loss of even a single species is not just an ecological event—it is a loss of a unique manifestation of divine artistry.

Animal testing raises further questions about the limits of necessity and the sanctity of life. While some scholars have historically allowed the use of animals in cases of legitimate need—such as medicine or disease research—there is an ethical threshold that cannot be crossed. Causing pain or death without clear justification contravenes Islamic values. The Prophet Muhammad (peace be upon him) once advised his companions to never use a living creature as a target for entertainment. This sensitivity to the emotional and physical suffering of animals requires Muslims today to scrutinize industries that rely on such practices and to advocate for alternatives wherever possible.

Climate change is not often framed as an animal issue, yet it deeply affects non-human life. As temperatures rise and natural disasters increase, animal habitats are destroyed, migration patterns disrupted, and food sources diminished. Islamic ethics, with its call for *mīzān*—balance—and *amana*—trust—demands that these changes not be ignored. Environmental degradation impacts animals as much as humans, and Islamic teachings place equal moral weight on preventing harm across species.

In Muslim-majority societies, there is often a disconnect between religious values and practice. Stray animals may suffer from neglect or abuse in public spaces. Urban development frequently displaces wildlife with no consideration for relocation or preservation. Religious leaders and scholars have an opportunity to bridge this gap by reviving neglected aspects of prophetic tradition and speaking to modern audiences about animal rights not as a Western import, but as an Islamic imperative.

Education remains one of the most effective tools. In mosques, schools, and homes, the legacy of mercy must be actively taught. Children who grow up hearing stories of the Prophet's care for animals will be less likely to contribute to cruelty. Institutions can play a role as well—by ensuring animal welfare laws are enforced, by funding shelters and clinics, and by supporting ethical farming initiatives rooted in Islamic principles.

Islamic responses to modern challenges must be rooted in both tradition and awareness of contemporary contexts. The tools are already present in scripture and legal discourse: the call to avoid harm, to act with compassion, and to uphold justice in all dealings. What is needed now is a translation of these values into action—through policy, personal choice, and collective effort.

Chapter 17: A Future of Compassion

In many ways, the ethical treatment of animals has emerged as one of the most important litmus tests of human civilization. As industrial progress continues to reshape the landscape of everyday life, the way communities respond to the presence and well-being of non-human creatures becomes a reflection of their moral priorities. Within the Islamic tradition, the foundation for such a response already exists—deeply rooted, spiritually sound, and resonant with contemporary calls for justice.

Youth-led initiatives in Muslim communities around the world have begun to address the disconnect between Islamic ideals and current practices. In cities across Southeast Asia and the Middle East, grassroots animal shelters are being established not just to house strays, but to educate the public on the rights animals have under divine law. These initiatives draw on hadiths that speak of reward for giving water to a thirsty dog, and warnings about cruelty to a caged cat—stories that had once been relegated to religious classes but are now emerging as calls to action.

Digital platforms have become unlikely but powerful vehicles for compassion. Social media campaigns raise awareness about animal cruelty, environmental destruction, and the ethical consumption of food. Young Muslims are increasingly asking questions their grandparents never needed to: Should halal meat come from a factory farm? Can synthetic leather be a more ethical alternative in Islamic fashion? What role should mosques play in promoting animal welfare?

Islamic schools and seminaries are slowly incorporating animal ethics into curricula once dominated by abstract jurisprudence. The ethical dimension of Islamic law is being explored more deeply, with scholars emphasizing that halal is not just a legal stamp, but a moral orientation. Veterinary ethics, once overlooked, is gaining attention in light of Islamic teachings on the treatment of sick and injured animals.

Mosques are beginning to explore their potential as centers for eco-spirituality. Rainwater harvesting systems, small garden plots, and awareness programs for children blend theology with practical environmentalism. In these spaces, care for the earth and its animals is not an extracurricular concern—it is part of worship, a visible expression of faith.

Conversations about animal rights are evolving. No longer limited to food and farming, they now touch on travel, tourism, and technology. The ethics of wildlife photography, the morality of keeping exotic pets, and even the implications of artificial intelligence in managing ecosystems are being examined through the lens of Qur'anic values. The idea that animals have agency, purpose, and place is guiding more nuanced perspectives than ever before.

At the heart of these developments is a return to an older, quieter wisdom. The kind that once led farmers to rest their beasts on the Sabbath, or inspired travelers to feed birds before setting out on long journeys. This kind of compassion was not theoretical—it was embodied, practiced, and passed down through generations. It treated mercy not as a concept, but as a lifestyle.

The modern Muslim is rediscovering this legacy, not in opposition to science or activism, but as a foundation for both.

The prophetic way offers not only stories but strategies—a lived theology that refuses to ignore suffering, whether it belongs to a human being or a silent creature in a field.

www.ingramcontent.com/pod-product-compliance
Ingram Content Group UK Ltd.
Pitfield, Milton Keynes, MK11 3LW, UK
UKHW011458200625
6509UKWH00030B/131